SACAGAWEA:

THE HEROINE OF DISCOVERY

by: **Mike McCraw**

Explorer, interpreter, guide, and naturalist; Sacagawea was a **19th century Shoshone woman** who was an important part of helping Thomas Jefferson's **Corps of Discovery Expedition** explore the western United States after the **Louisiana Purchase**.

Sacagawea was born in **May of 1788** to the chief of the **Lemhi Shoshone tribe** in an area now known as **Salmon, Idaho**.

1788

In **1800**, 12 year old Sacagawea was **kidnapped by the Hidatsa tribe** during a raid of her Shoshone village.

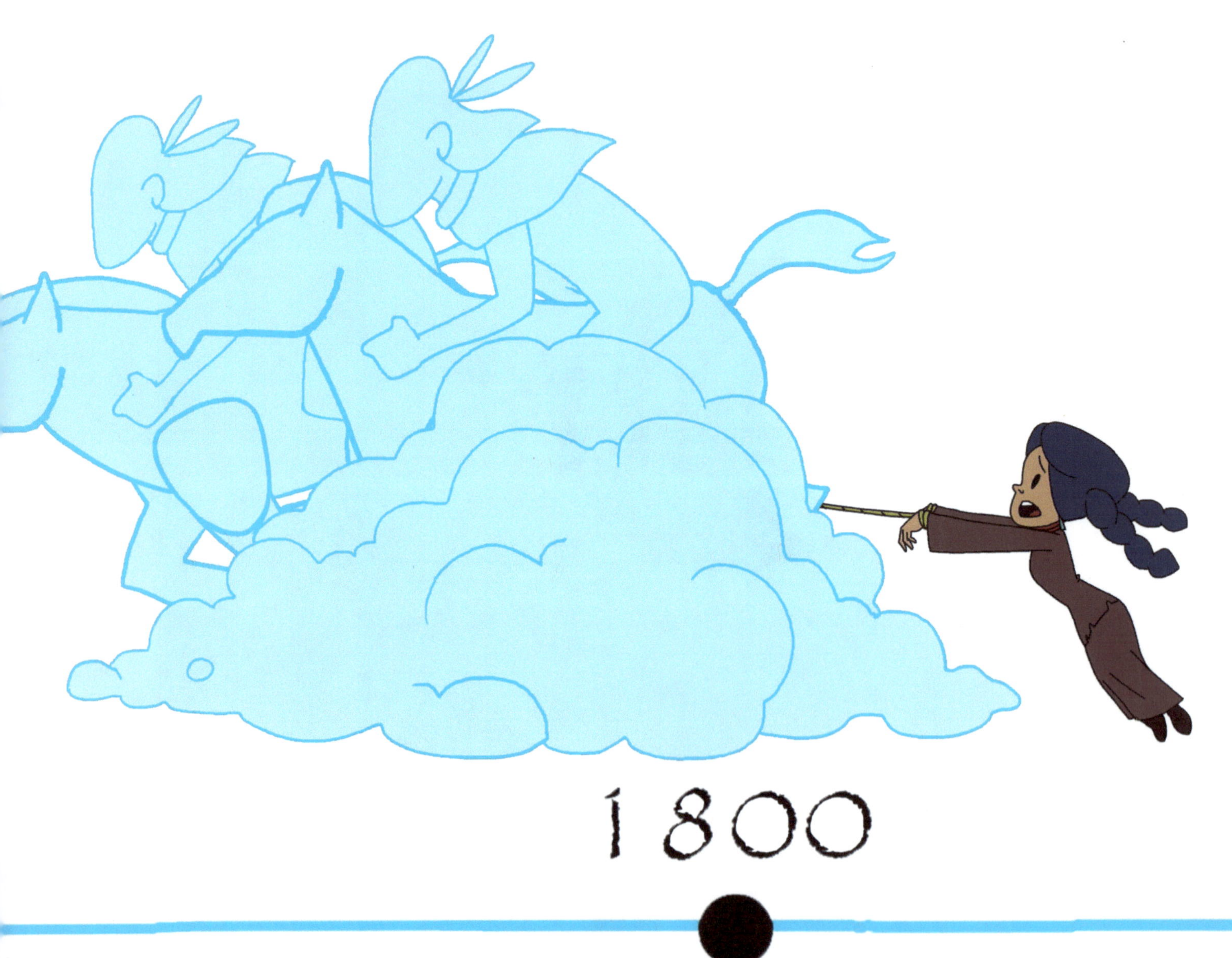

As a captive of the Hidatsa, Sacagawea mainly **farmed** and **tended to the homes of her abductors**.

The year was **1804** when Sacagawea met a French-Canadian fur trader named **Toussaint Charbonneau** who had begun living with the Hidatsa people at the time.

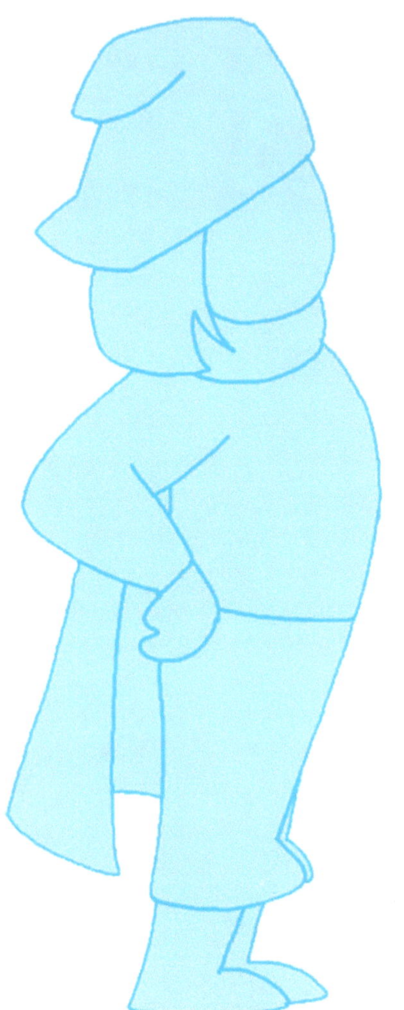

1804

Shortly after meeting, they were married. Not only was Toussaint **21 years older** than her...

...but also, it is believed, Tousaint either **bought** the young, 16 year old Sacagawea or **won** her as gambling winnings.
Definitely not the greatest love story ever told.

Later on, that same year, **Sacagawea became pregnant** with her first child.

In **November of 1804**, Sacagawea and Toussaint hear of a group of U.S army volunteers who set up camp nearby, named the **Corps of Discovery**, looking to hire translators and guides for their expedition west.

A year earlier, in **1803**, the United States purchased close to **827,000 sq. miles** of land from France known as the **Louisiana Purchase**.

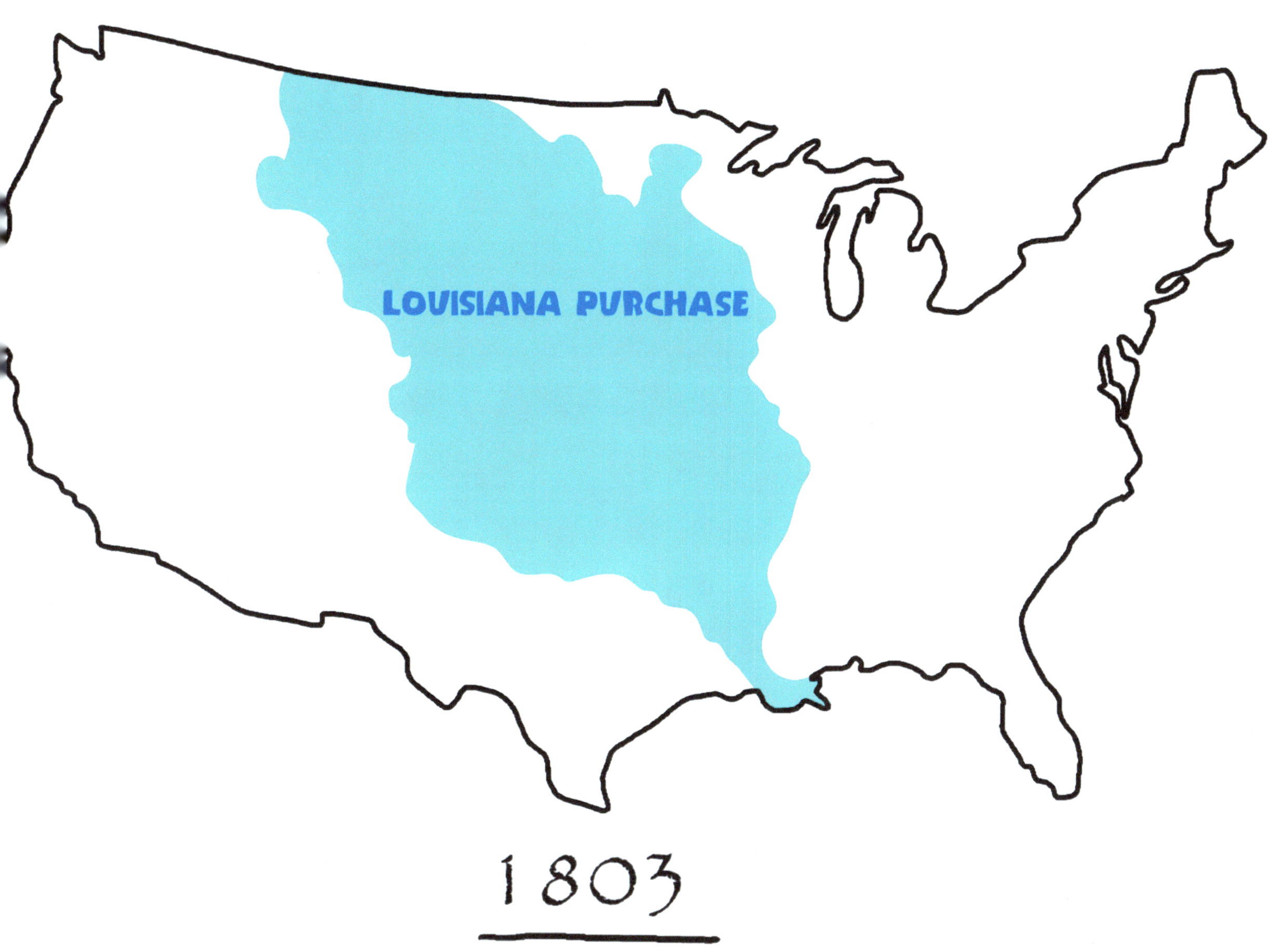

Unable to officially explore this land before, President Thomas Jefferson commissioned **Meriwether Lewis** and **William Clark** to form the **Corps of Discovery** and venture off into this territory, **exploring the nature and people** of the newly acquired land.

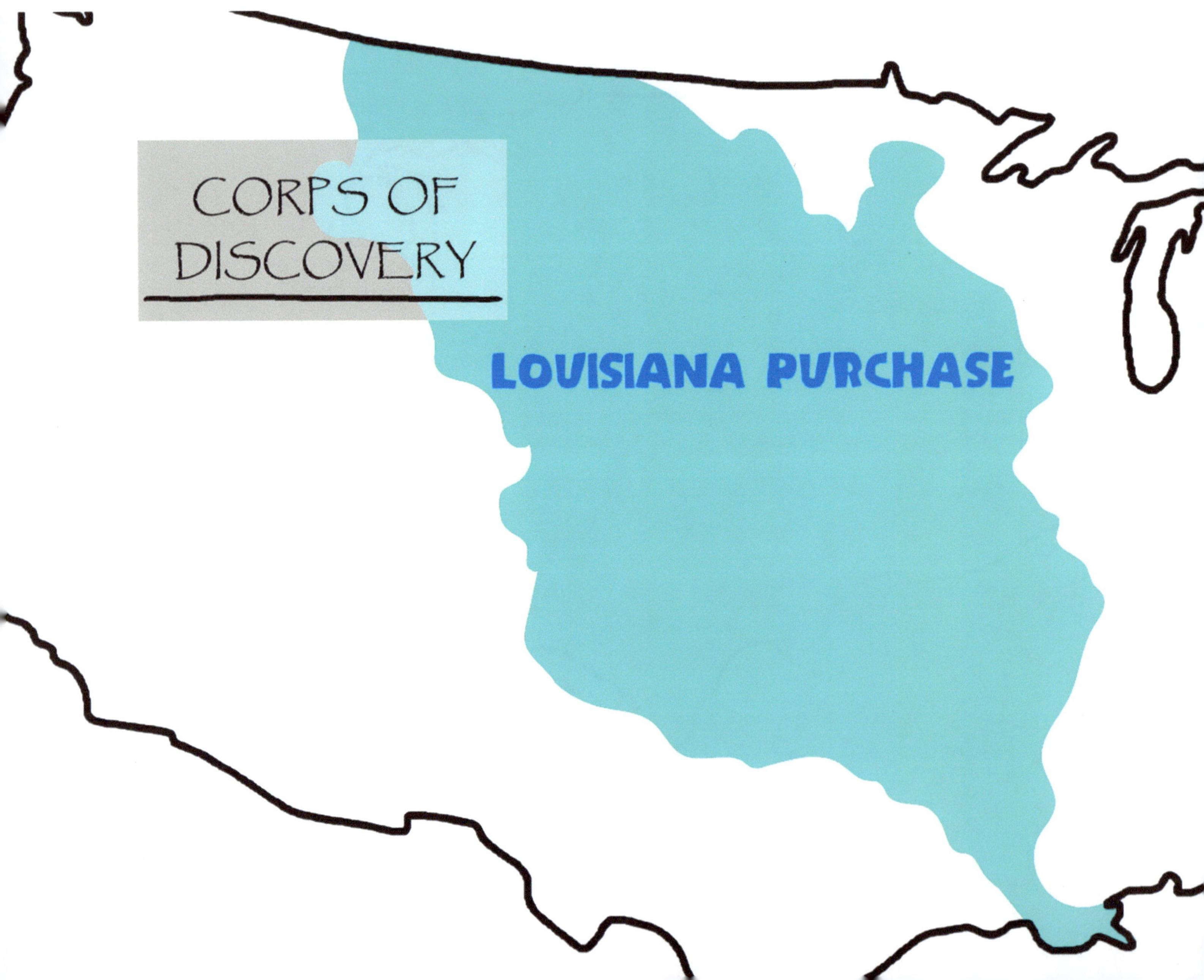

The expedition started in **St. Louis** and set up camp in the **Mandan Village** where they named their camp...well...**Camp Mandan**.

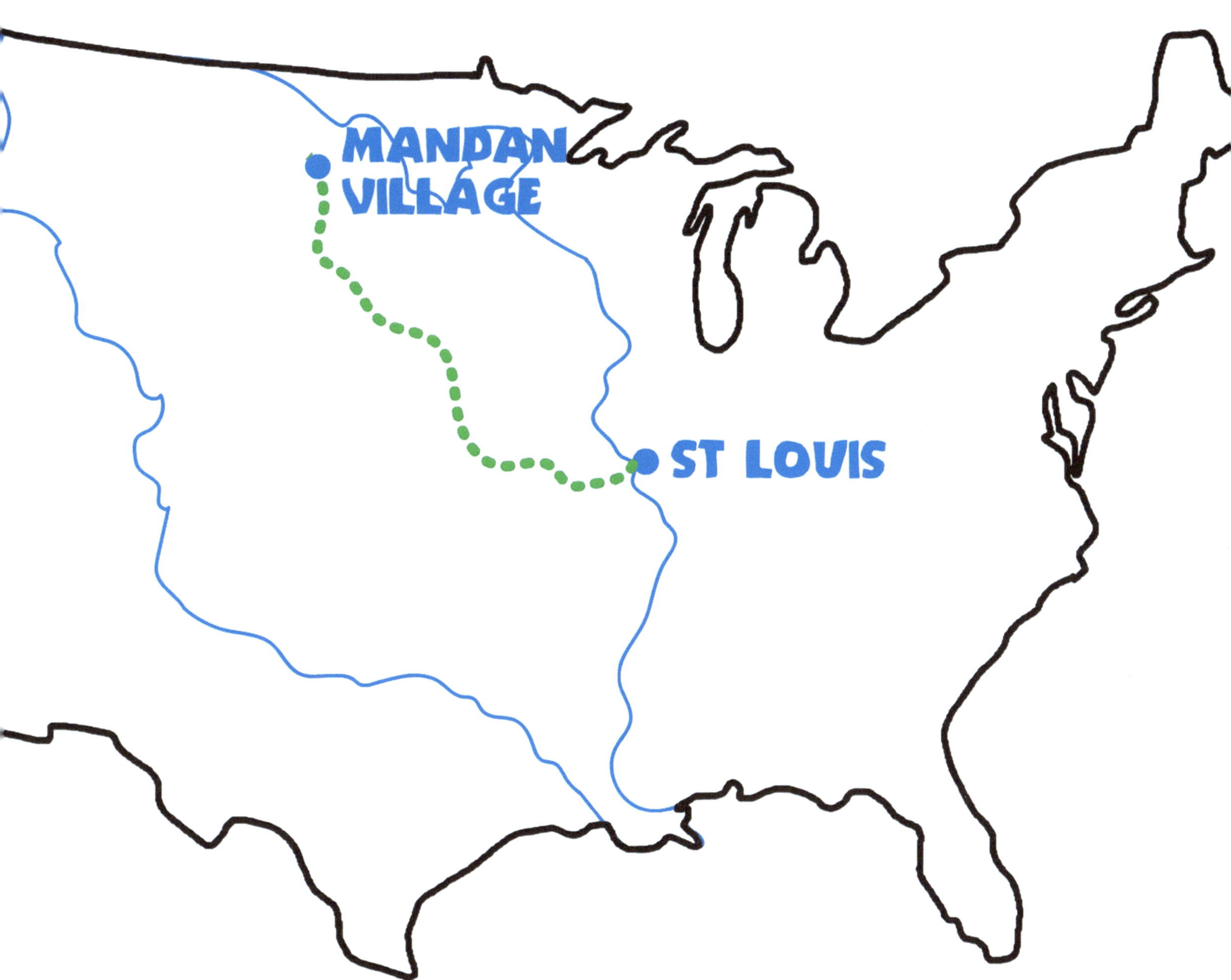

Toussaint brought Sacagawea with him to the camp, interested in getting the translator job for himself. Which he got. After the commanders, Lewis and Clark, met Sacagawea.

Though pregnant, Lewis and Clark felt this young Shoshone woman's involvement with the difficult expedition was key, for **peaceful interactions** and **clear communication** with native tribes they would encounter.

On **February 11, 1805**, just a few months before they were to set out on the expedition, Sacagawea gave birth to her son, **Jean Baptiste Charbonneau**.

1805

On **April 7, 1805**, Sacagawea and her family left the Mandan village to accompany the Corps of Discovery on their expedition by way of the **Missouri River.** They used smaller, canoe-like boats known as **pirogues**.

1805

It was on **May 14, 1805** when, due to high winds, the waves began to pick up and the boat containing Sacagawea and her family nearly capsized.

1805

As the bowman and crew struggled to steady the boat, a level-headed and composed Sacagawea rescued important **journals, papers, and scientific instruments** from the river.

The Corps was grateful as so much of their journey would have been wasted had it not been for Sacagawea's forward thinking. They insisted this section of the Missouri River be named, the **Sacagawea River**.

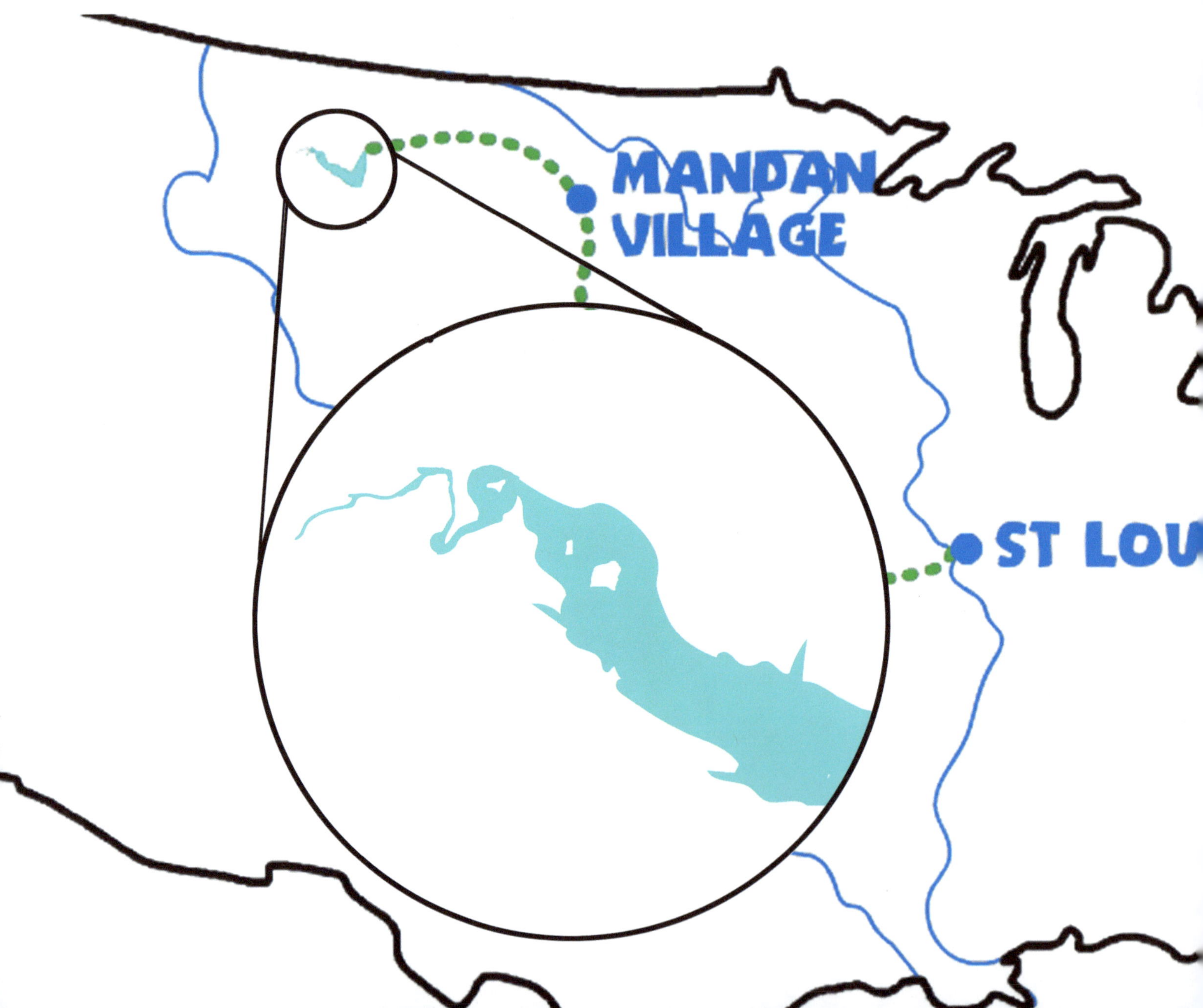

Sadly, Sacagawea had come down with an unknown illness that caused her **intense pelvic pain** and a **terrible fever**.

Lewis and Clark began to help nurse her back to health with a treatment of **tree bark compress** over her stomach, **opium**, and **mineral water**.

A good ten days later, Sacagawea was back to good health and able to fully continue working with the Corps as **forager**, **guide**, and **interpreter**.

As the expedition approached the Rocky Mountains, Lewis took three men to scout ahead on a route known as the **Lemhi Pass** and encountered the, not-so inviting, **Shoshone Tribe**.

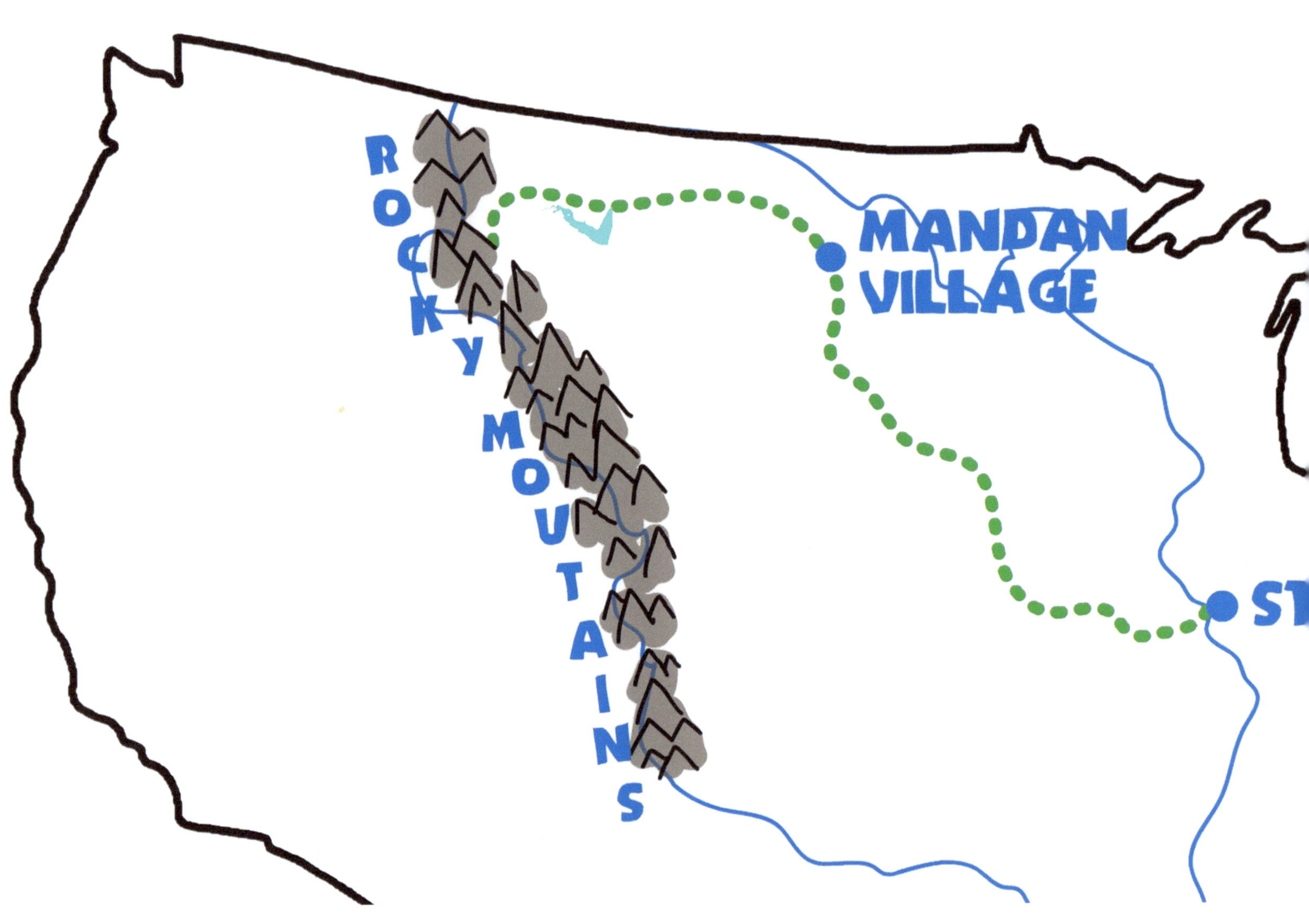

Knowing Sacagawea spoke Shoshone, Lewis worked hard to encourage the **Shoshone chief**, **Cameahwait** to head east and meet with their interpreter. He hoped to trade for horses that would help the Corps cross the Rocky Mountains.

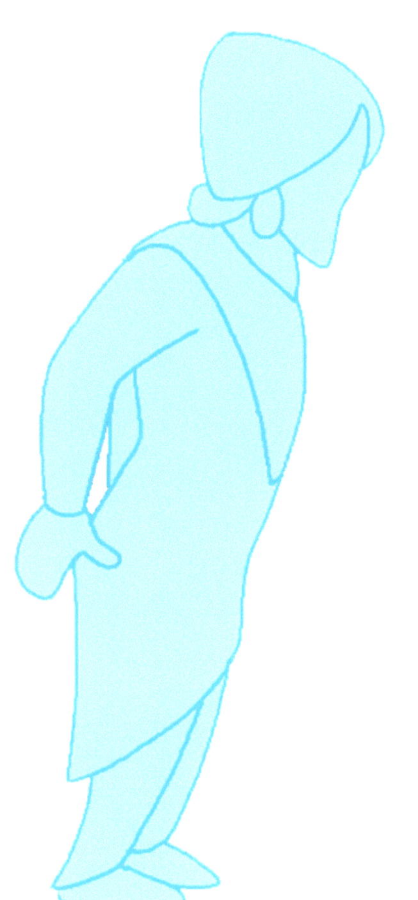

Sacagawea and Chief Cameahwait got more than they bargained for at this meeting when they immediately recognized one another. **Chief Cameahwait was Sacagawea's older brother** who had taken over as chief of her tribe of birth.

The reunion was not only heart warming for Sacagawea but also very beneficial for the Corps. They got the **horses** they were hoping for, but also gained **guides** who lead them through the gates of the Rocky Mountains.

The journey over the Rocky Mountains was rough. definitely the roughest part of an already strenuous journey. The **weather**, **terrain**, **and lack of food** weighed on the Corps heavily. The crew were so hungry that they resorted to eating candles that were made out of beef fat known as **tallow**.

On **September 22, 1805**, the Corps of Discovery successfully made it to the other side of the Rocky Mountains.

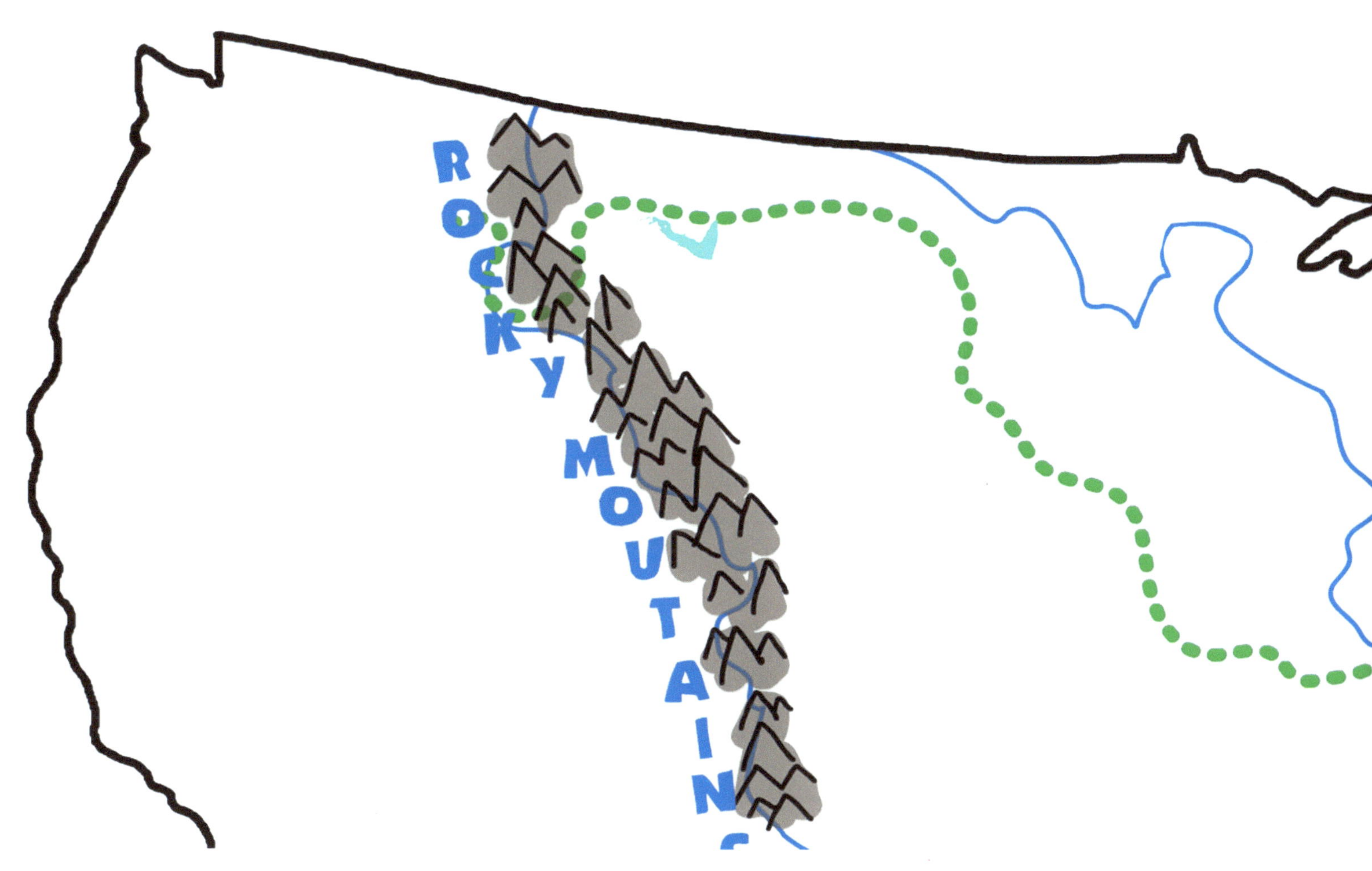

Sagawea was integral in helping the crew regain their strength by finding edible plants for everyone to eat.

As they continued west, Sacagawea remained an important guide and translator. Even, at one point, negotiating a trade with a native woman for a sea otter fur coat as a gift for President Thomas Jefferson, himself.

The expedition came to an end in December of **1805** when **the Corps of Discovery reached the Pacific west coast**. The Corps set up camp which they called **Fort Clatsop** after the nearby Clatsop natives who tipped them off about the area. This is where they waited out the winter until breaking up camp on **March 23, 1806**.

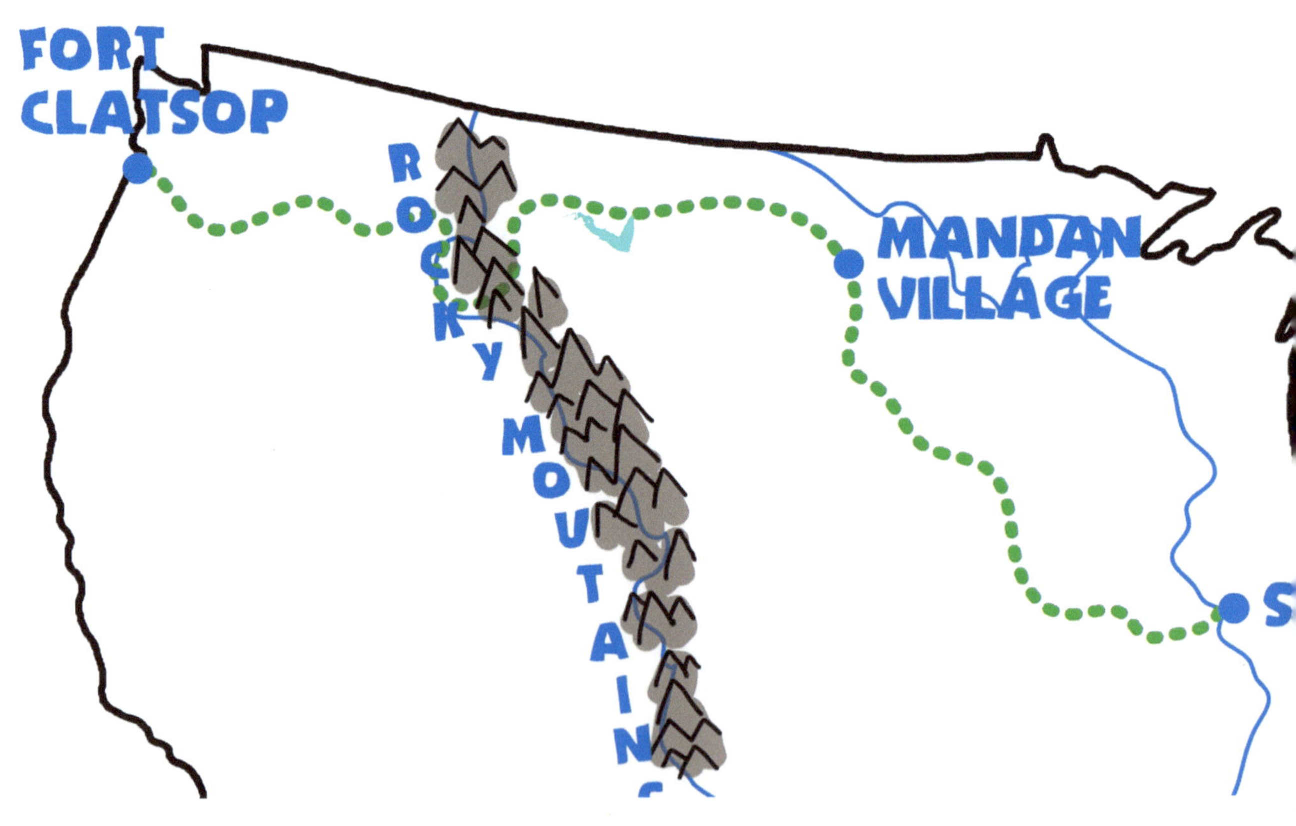

Lewis and Clark both took seperate routes back to St. Louis. Sacagawea and her family went with Clark who they became extremely close to on the expedition. So close that, in **1809,** they accepted a patch of land in Missouri and enrolled their son, Jean Baptistse, in St. Louis Academy.

1809

Apparently, farm life in Missouri didn't work out for them and they gave full custody of Jean Baptiste to William Clark right before **leaving for Fort Manuel Lisa, South Dakota.**

Details on Sacagawea are hazy after leaving St. Louis except that she **died on August 14th, 1812 of putrid fever at the age of 24**. She left behind an infant daughter, **Lizette Charbonneau,** who's fate is also still a mystery.

1812

In the year **2000**, the **U.S Treasury decided to put Sacagawea's image on a newly designed $1 coin** to commemorate her importance to the discovery of the United States as we now know it.

2000

Generosity, cooperation, poise, and friendship are all things seemingly important to and characteristic of the heroine of discovery, **Sacagawea**. This is just a small peek into what is known and currently being discovered about the woman, **Sacagawea and her timeline**.

www.ingramcontent.com/pod-product-compliance
Lightning Source LLC
LaVergne TN
LVHW070201110826
845147LV00002B/464
* 9 7 8 0 5 7 8 4 8 5 8 3 6 *